"Selling your winners and holding your losers is like cutting the flowers and watering the woods." - Peter Lynch

The Intelligent Investor's Art of Selling

Master Stock Selling Strategies, Manage Risk, Minimize Regrets, and Maximize Profits to Build Wealth

BALAJI KASAL

WWW.BALAJIKASAL.COM

Copyright © 2024 by Balaji Kasal

All rights reserved. No part of this book or publication may be reproduced, transmitted, or stored in any form or by any means – including mechanical, electronic, photocopying, recording, or any information storage and retrieval - without written permission from the author.

Contact: info@balajikasal.com

On Mission @The Intelligent Investors Hub

www.intelligentinvestorshub.com

To those ready to master the art of taking money off the table to succeed.

May I Ask You a Favor?

I would like to hear your thoughts about my book and book series – 'The Intelligent Investor's'. *Please leave a review on the platforms from you bought the book.*

It serves two purposes: first, it helps me understand what areas you want to master in the investment game, and second, it improves my craft for you.

Sincerely,

Thank You.

Balaji Kasal

Your Free Gift!

As a token of my **thank you** for taking out time to read the book and also for leaving a review.

Download your Free eBook pdf copy.

Alternatively, click:

https://balaji-kasal.ck.page/cb67feb275

TABLE OF CONTENT

PREFACE 7

1 INTRODUCTION 13

    1.1   SELLING: A PERSPECTIVE 15
    1.2   COMMON SELLING STRATEGIES 19
    1.3   COMMON MYTHS AND MISTAKES IN SELLING 21

2 THE ROLE OF EMOTIONAL INTELLIGENCE IN SELLING 33

    2.1   EMOTIONAL BIAS BARRIERS 34
    2.2   CULTIVATE THE RIGHT MINDSET 47

3 MASTER *WHY* BEHIND EVERY SELL 53

    3.2   YOUR ROLE - YOUR MARKET EDGE 56
    3.3   THE IMPORTANCE OF SELLING 61
    3.4   WHY SELLING IS HARDER AND RISKIER? 65

4 MASTER THE RIGHT SELL TIME – *WHEN?* . 69

    4.1   REVISITING THE INITIAL PURCHASE DECISION 71
    4.2   STRATEGIC SELLING 72
    4.3   KEY QUESTIONS BEFORE SELLING 74

5 RULES FOR SELLING AS AN INVESTOR 77

6 RULES FOR SELLING AS A TRADER 125

7 CONCLUSION 169

8 ALL SELL RULES IN ONE PLACE 173

8.1	RULES FOR SELLING AS AN INVESTOR	173
8.2	RULES FOR SELLING AS A TRADER	176

9   GLOSSARY OF SPECIFIC TERMS 179

10   BIBLIOGRAPHY 181

11   BOOK SERIES – "THE INTELLIGENT INVESTOR'S" 182

THE INTELLIGENT INVESTORS HUB 188

Preface

"Learn every day, but especially from the experiences of others. It's cheaper!"

– Jack Welch

With over two decades in the stock market, I began with mutual funds before moving on to direct equity trading. Over time, I realized that long-term investment is key to wealth creation. Today, I am financially independent and help others achieve the same as ***mission***.

Each phase of my journey presented different challenges and opportunities. I learned from books, articles, videos, social media and everything I get to. I studied legendary investors worldwide, noting their styles, how they seized opportunities, and how they reacted to adversity.

In the stock market, everyone faces tough situations and makes mistakes – buying the wrong stocks, buying too little, or selling too soon. Through my experiences, I discovered that selling is often the most overlooked yet *crucial*. This realization led me to write the book, where I share rules and strategies for making sound selling decisions.

> *Selling is riskier than buying; those who understand it build lasting wealth in the stock market.*

Selling is tricky, leaving many unsure or confused. This book provides essential golden rules to help you make informed decisions to maximize wealth.

I aim to offer a broad view of selling and strategies to help you decide when to sell fully, partially, or not at all. Market actions require a firm mindset and guiding rules, which this book will cover.

Remember, you only realize a profit or loss when executing the sale transaction. This is the **ultimate realization of your capital's return.** Until then, it remains under the influence of market forces, and its value fluctuates according to market participants' sentiments and the current or anticipated performance of the underlying business.

Layout of This Book

The book is not intended to be read in a hurry. The ideas here require careful reflection to be effectively applied. To support this, ample space is given to explore concepts fully, allowing you to absorb and internalize each idea comfortably.

The spacious book pages slow down reading speed so that your thoughts get provoked effectively.

This approach will provide you with ***clarity on why and when to sell a business or a stock.*** The book is designed to enhance understanding and encourage thoughtful action so that you can decide to sell on your terms rather than under pressure. Viewing it from this perspective will help you preserve and grow your wealth, setting you toward financial independence.

Finally, you may notice some repetition throughout the book. This is intentional, as it can reinforce the perspective shifts necessary for a successful mindset. Revisiting ideas helps program your subconscious mind to make effective decisions when the time is right. Comprehending these concepts fully is more impactful than reading quickly; it allows you to maximize available opportunities. ***Remember, each sell or not to sell is an***

opportunity presented to you to grow your net worth.

I recommend revisiting the key concepts regularly to effectively use the 'sell' option when needed.

1 Introduction

"Life's battles don't always go to the strongest or fastest; sooner or later, those who win are those who think they can."

– Richard Bach

As a market participant, you have only four options:

1. Not to Buy

2. Buy

3. Not to Sell (Hold)

4. Sell

Beyond these, you must also consider additional factors: what to buy, how much capital to allocate, how long to hold, at which price to buy, at what price to sell, when to sell, and how much to sell.

Up to this point, your focus may have been primarily on what and when to buy.

This process has strong aspects on its side:

1. Storytelling an opportunity

2. Number-crunching down to the last digits of price and value

3. Following various charts and patterns

These powerful tools open a fascinating world with endless potential for creating stories and themes. Number crunching is especially favored by academics who enjoy working with formulas and theories. It is easy to teach and can stretch students' intellectual limits, even when the problem has little real-world relevance.

In today's digital world, analyzing price charts for stocks and indices is simpler than ever. Building narratives and variables around these charts is tempting, but it often overlooks the real business risks, our own goals, and the challenges involved.

1.1 Selling: A Perspective

Selling is a personal game you need to master, and as you go through this book, you will see *why*. Your decision to sell either brings profits into your account or leaves money on the table.

Remember, *selling is trickier than buying; it is more of an art form that allows you to maximize your gains or limit your losses.*

As an investor, you buy a piece of business based on your framework, understanding companies within your competence circle.

As a trader, you buy company stock based on various strategies but to sell at a future date.

Must be remembered that, ***when someone buys with selling in mind, it becomes a trade or speculation.***

For instance, you might spot a gap between a business's price and value (Margin of Safety). A corporate event, such as a merger or spinoff, could also lead you to buy, anticipating a sale at a higher price or value. It is *a trade taught as 'cigar-butt' investing*.

Meanwhile, a speculator keeps life busy by following stock price, volume momentum, trends, and the full gamut of emotions, taking the person easily on a fantasy journey.

As an investor, you can choose which stock to buy, at what price, and quantity. Once you buy a stock, you become partial owner of the business. From there, you have two options: to sell or not to sell (hold). You can also sell part of your holdings and keep the rest based on *your own discretion*.

It is essential to be crystal clear about your selling strategies. ***These rules should be established before you buy; otherwise, you may be forced to sell under undesirable conditions, potentially resulting in losses or missed future gains.***

Remember, you make money when you sell in the market. Until then, gains or losses sit in your account and may not be realized as you expect. In this book, we will explore different strategies for effective selling.

The trick lies in your ability to sell to book the profit, cut losses, or seize a better opportunity. Selling is more of an art; to complete the picture, you must design your selling strategies as an integral part of your approach. In other words, *completing the buying, holding, and selling cycle is essential to maximizing profits and building wealth.*

Like buying, selling comes with emotional challenges, such as greed and fear. Investors and traders must be aware of their emotions, biases, hidden mistakes, and risk exposure.

Using technical analysis, a chartist relies on the psychology and sentiments of market participants. *The underlying assumption here is that everyone's emotions and behavior when buying or selling will resemble past patterns. This speculative perspective attracts chartists to use various techniques to sell and expect to profit.* We must remember the standard disclaimer by fund houses – *'the past performance is not necessarily indicative of the future performance.*

1.2 Common Selling Strategies

Let's briefly review the broad selling strategies used by various market participants:

1. **Fundamental Analysis:** Selling based on deteriorating financials and the lack of visible improvement in the future.

2. **Event-Driven Selling:** This is triggered by corporate or industry environment changes that negatively impact the business's prospects. For example, a considered acquisition in an unrelated field can harm business valuation.

3. **Technical Analysis Selling Triggers:** A chartist uses predefined techniques to decide when to sell, such as a breakout below a support level or a drop in momentum

indicators like the Moving Average Convergence Divergence (MACD) or Relative Strength Index (RSI) and so forth.

4. **Selling Based on Quantitative Analysis:** In today's digital era, machines use various algorithms to detect trends, correlations, predictive indicators in price patterns, market analyses, and other quantifiable data to take decision on sell.

5. **Statistical Arbitrage (Pair Trading):** This strategy involves taking a short position in one stock while simultaneously going long in another correlated one. It relies on meticulous analysis to exploit valuation discrepancies. It could be any correlated securities like stocks, indices, gold, oil, commodities and so forth.

This leads us to understand what all common myths market participants have that cause them tend to mistakes.

1.3 Common Myths and Mistakes in Selling

In the stock market, participants aim to profit and build wealth. However, a critical aspect often overlooked is that gains are only realized when the ***sell*** transaction is executed. Otherwise, the paper profit based on stock price movement is not tangible. Technically, this is known as Mark-to-Market (MTM) accounting, and it fluctuates with stock price movements.

Thus, your actual profit is only realized when you sell. Many myths, followed blindly, can confuse people during the selling process and lead to common mistakes. Such behaviors often reflect a lack of understanding of the investment or trading process and can result in mediocre returns, losses, or missed opportunities to benefit from the magic of compounding.

Here are some widely observed myths about selling in the stock market:

Myth No. 1: Buy Low and Sell High.

Mistake: This mentality often leads to buying a mediocre company simply because the price is low, hoping it will rise. This blind spot assumes that a low stock price cannot go lower, which can be costly.

Myth No. 2: Buy at the Bottom and Sell at the Top.

Mistake: This is wishful thinking and, in reality, nearly impossible to achieve consistently. If someone manages this as a single transaction, it is due to luck, not a repeatable strategy. Waiting for the bottom often means missing out on profitable investments, and it is equally difficult to pinpoint the exact top to sell.

Myth No. 3: Sell the Stock When Its Price Appreciates by some percentages say, 10%, 15%, 20%, or 25%.

Mistake: Fixing a return percentage as a selling point is usually a mistake because a stock could have multi-bagger potential based on its fundamentals. While some investors may feel comfortable selling at a set profit, this approach breaks the compounding effect and raises truncation costs.

Myth No. 4: Sell if the Stock Drops below the Buying Price.

Mistake: The stock does not know the price you paid for it. Panicking and selling solely because the cost of shares has fallen shows a lack of research and conviction.

Myth No. 5: Sell Now if the Stock Price Drops some percentages say, 5%, 10%, 20%, or 30%.

Mistake: This myth is a corollary of Myth No. 4. The key difference is that the decision to sell is based on a specific percentage drop rather than the company's underlying potential. This approach overlooks the importance of evaluating the business fundamentals.

Myth No. 6: Follow the 7% Sell Rule: If the stock falls 7% or more from the entry price, it triggers the sell decision.

Mistake: This specific guideline encourages speculative behavior among investors. Such mechanical rules often benefit brokers more than the investors themselves.

Myth No. 7: There is Negative News About the Company; Now Is the Time to Sell.

Mistake: Companies inevitably go through cycles, including challenging periods. The decision to sell should be based on the company's capacity to recover from adversity, which is essential for long-term investment success.

Myth No. 8: Economic Decline Means It is Time to Sell Owned Stocks.

Mistake: Making a sell decision solely based on the prevailing economic scenario is often misguided. Investments are made in specific businesses, not the whole economy. A temporary regional economic slowdown may not significantly affect certain companies, like those in essential goods, luxury items, or import-export to growth markets.

Myth No. 9: Sell Now to Buy Back at a Lower Price in the Future.

Mistake: A typical trader when sees a rise in stock price, rush to sell and lock in profits, hoping the stock price will drop, allowing them to repurchase it for less. If it is a high-quality business, selling just because the price has risen can be a mistake, as it misses the potential for long-term compounding.

Myth No. 10: Sell the Stock if Quarterly Earnings Do Not Meet Expectations.

Mistake: Many market participants have a short-term view, closely tracking earnings reports. Any dip in expectations can trigger a sale. However, it is crucial to investigate the reasons behind lower-than-expected revenue growth to understand whether it is a temporary or long-term issue before deciding to sell.

Myth No. 11: When the Stock Market Crashes, Sell and Exit (Panic-Selling). Reenter Once Volatility Reduces.

Mistake: The stock market is meant to serve you, especially when fear causes widespread selling. This volatility can present opportunities to buy stock at lower prices. For an investor, instability is a friend that allows capital to be deployed more effectively.

Myth No. 12: Sell if a Celebrity Investor Has Exited from the Company Stock.

Mistake: While studying celebrity investors can provide valuable insights into investment principles and trading strategies, blindly following their actions can be a mistake. They frequently manage large populations, have a different universe of opportunities, and may have reasons for selling that are not publicly known. Always do your homework and follow your investment framework and strategies.

Myth No. 13: If a Stock Has Not Moved for a Few Months or Even a

Couple of Years, It Must Be a Bad Company, So Sell It.

<u>Mistake:</u> Some stocks remain undiscovered by market participants, causing their prices to stagnate for extended periods. Patience is essential as long as the business fundamentals are strong and showing growth. The stock market does not operate based on our timing or needs. In such cases, you might consider buying more shares. Eventually, the market will recognize the underlying business value and growth potential. It lead you to ride on bumper profit and wealth.

Myth No. 14: My Mood Is Not Good Today, So Sell.

<u>Mistake:</u> Emotions play a significant role in the market, but letting personal feelings dictate transactions is a mistake. Remember, the market is unaware of your emotions.

Myth No. 15: My Neighbor Is Getting Rich with Rising Stock, So I Will Sell My Existing Holdings and Buy What They Own to Get Rich Quickly.

Mistake: Envy is an even greater behavioral anomaly in the stock market than greed and fear. ***Remember, investing is a personal journey.*** You need to follow your framework to reach your goals. Your progress in investing should be compared only to your past achievements, not anyone else's.

Myth No. 16: A Technical Chart Showing a Lower High and Lower Low is a Definite Sell Signal.

Mistake: Technical analysis occasionally benefits a trader but does not necessarily produce long-term wealth.

Myth No. 17: I Hold Only a Small Number of Shares in a Great Company, So I will Sell and Book the Profit.

<u>Mistake:</u> Holding even a small number of shares in a wonderful business that compounded your capital is beneficial. The power of compounding can build a substantial wealth over time. In such cases, an intelligent investor might consider buying more shares.

<u>Myth No. 18: I Have Been Holding Company Shares for Over 2-3 years, and I Am Bored. I Should Sell Now.</u>

<u>Mistake:</u> Investing can be a long, often uneventful process. Even an emotionally intelligent investor with an average Intelligent Quotient (IQ) can achieve great results by patiently compounding wealth over time. The stock market is not meant for entertainment or excitement.

<u>Myth No. 19: I Need to Lower My Tax Burden, So I Will Sell Now.</u>

<u>Mistake:</u> Selling solely to manage taxes rarely contributes to wealth building. Unless selling aligns with

short-term financial goals or makes strategic sense, it is usually better to hold an investment to compound.

Myth No. 20: Reduce Risk by *Diversifying* and Selling Stocks to Adjust the Portfolio.

Mistake: This is *one of the most misguided arguments in investing*. Diversifying just for the sake of it is a mistake. An intelligent investor should build a portfolio of businesses aligned with own objectives and risk tolerance.

These are a few major myths you must be aware. So that, associated mistakes could be eliminated for your successful investment journey.

*****

2 The Role of Emotional Intelligence in Selling

"To buy when others are despondently selling and sell when others are greedily buying requires the greatest fortitude and pays the greatest reward."

— John Templeton

Emotions and past experiences heavily influence human decisions and actions. While historical events may not always apply directly to a current situation, we are often conditioned to react based on them.

Emotions tend to be spontaneous and can lead to impulsive decisions. Therefore, developing emotional intelligence and stability is essential for successfully navigating the investment journey.

Buying, holding or selling in the stock market requires objectivity and rational thinking. Remember, as a market participant, you are responsible for making decisions today that lead to favorable outcomes in the future. Rationality stems from a sense of balance, which calms the mind and nurtures the ability to make effective decisions based on facts, personal goals, risk tolerance, and judgment.

This is why I emphasize emotional mastery and rational thinking. These are the keys to a successful, long-term investment journey, enabling you to benefit from compounding and build enduring wealth.

Everything starts with you, so in the following sections, let us recognize personal biases and work toward cultivating the right mindset.

2.1   Emotional Bias Barriers

Here are a few key emotions to recognize and guard against to help you avoid unnecessary risks in the stock market.

1. Instant Gratification

A common emotional response to investing is the urge to sell immediately and pocket the profit. *Humans naturally prefer immediate rewards over waiting for a potentially better outcome, and the desire for instant gratification is a major reason many people settle for mediocre results.*

Delayed gratification, on the other hand, requires patience - holding a well-performing stock with conviction and waiting for the right investment opportunities. In the stock market, instant gratifications transfer wealth from impatient participants to those with patience and preparation. Focus on generating strong investment ideas and trust your process. Have the patience to buy a high-quality business at an attractive price and to hold onto long-term compounders rather than selling too soon.

2. Greed and Fear

The desire for more often traps us in a cycle of greed, not just for money but for anything that brings pleasure. Conversely, our basic survival instincts trigger fear — fear of loss, whether of love, respect, money, or other valued assets.

In the stock market, people often believe they can outsmart the crowd and fall into the trap of *'buy low and sell high'* without considering the underlying business or the impact of market sentiment on prices. Fear takes hold when the market spirals downward, and participants become anxious to sell.

When prices rise, they speculate on two options:

1. Selling their holding to profit now, hoping to repurchase when prices drop, or
2. Buying at higher prices to follow the crowd.

This is a trap driven by greed to make money in every scenario. *An intelligent investor acts only when the gap between the price paid and the value offered is favorable.*

3. Envy

Envy is one of the dangerous emotions that can take control of the mind. It arises when a person is dissatisfied with what they have or feels it is insufficient. This bias leads individuals to desire what others possess.

In this situation, emotions can push a person into the trap of buying and selling quickly to make fast money, which is often the first step toward becoming prey to market fluctuations.

To combat this, develop the habit of adhering to your rule book. You would be better off, if you compete against your past Self. It would lead you to lasting success.

4. Anchoring Bias

Anchoring bias influences, us unconsciously, often leading investors to fixate on a specific buy or sell price. When we make the mistake of buying a poorly performing stock and its price subsequently drops below our purchase price, we tend to wait for it to rebound. In essence, we anchor ourselves to it.

In this scenario, multiple emotions and biases come into play, including anchoring, loss aversion, and denial. A rational response involves recognizing the mistake and having the courage to sell, which is a wise decision.

5. Overconfidence Bias

Overconfidence bias causes us to overrate our opinions and leads us into an overconfidence trap. This results in excessive optimism about a company and may lead us to pay a high price for its stock, thereby exposing us to greater risks.

Confidence is an essential trait in investing. However, becoming overconfident and ignoring changing facts can lead to trouble. Sales decisions should be based on a factual evaluation of the business's prospects.

Thus, it is vital to remain humble and agile to recognize facts rationally and act accordingly.

6. Confirmation Bias

When investors find a business attractive during their evaluation, they often conduct further research that mainly supports their initial investment thesis. Conversely, when even minor bad news about the company is reported, investors' views may shift dramatically, leading many to sell.

In this case, we mistakenly interpret the negative signal as confirmation of a permanent decline in the business, prompting us to sell the stock. However, the company may still have the potential to recover and grow.

A helpful strategy to guard against confirmation bias is to '*invert*' the case to gain new insights. Consider asking the following questions:

- To what extent could the future economics of the business be affected?

- Is the deterioration in business performance temporary, long-term, or permanent?

7. Authority Bias

We often regard certain individuals as authorities in their respective fields and tend to follow their lead. In the stock market, participants can be easily influenced by their actions. Many investors attempt to replicate the stock market transactions of these prominent figures, operating under the assumption that imitating a celebrity investor's choices will yield similar performance.

The issues with authority bias include:

1. Celebrity investors' investment styles and objectives may differ significantly from yours.

2. They often operate with much larger capital, which can change the dynamics of their opportunities.

3. They may sell to diversify into other asset classes, such as real

estate, which might not align with your goals.

4. They could possess a higher risk appetite than you are comfortable with.

5. Their investment time horizons may vary from yours.

While there is value in learning investment strategies and various approaches from these experienced investors, blindly following their every transaction can lead to unknown and undesirable situations.

Therefore, establishing your investment framework and selling strategies will help you make the best decisions for your unique circumstances.

6. Availability Miss-weighing Bias

Availability bias leads us to rely on readily available data, fitting it into our decision-making framework even if it is of little relevance from a long-term investment perspective. This behavior distorts our decision-making process and increases risk.

As an intelligent investor, examining each data point objectively and differentiating what is truly important from what is not is essential. Your selling decision should be based on objectivity and factual reasoning.

7. Psychological Denial Bias

Psychological denial bias occurs when we refuse to accept information that contradicts our investment preferences. We often resist being proven wrong, as it challenges our sense of self and can hurt our ego.

We frequently decide to wait and watch, even when the facts suggest a different narrative. Our investment thesis should focus on the business's prospects. Any changes in the underlying facts - such as declining business performance, management issues, or labor unrest - must be evaluated in the context of the company's long-term economic story. We must train our minds to make rational decisions about selling stock based on the evidence presented.

However, we can sometimes develop an emotional attachment to our owned stocks, leading to blind spots and an inability to recognize deteriorating conditions. This attachment can result in financial losses or poor performance.

8. Miss-gambling Compulsion Bias

The gambling bias compels us to trade and speculate excessively. Humans are drawn to activities that keep us engaged and give us the 'illusion' of accomplishment, often leading to impulsive decisions that prioritize short-term excitement over long-term strategy.

In the market, traders often become fascinated by volatility, attempting to capitalize on every movement. This behavior can lead to poor performance and high transaction costs. It is important to make a move only when you are in an advantageous position; otherwise, ignore the market fluctuations.

9. Commitment Bias

Also known as the endowment effect, commitment bias refers to our tendency to assign greater value to what we own. In behavioral science, this can manifest as a painful reluctance to relinquish possessions, leading to overconfidence and emotional attachment. We often resist acknowledging our mistakes or facing the possibility of being judged for them.

This bias is rooted in the idea that *"humans are not rational beings but rationalizing beings."* This means we are quick to justify our actions rather than objectively evaluate changing facts or acknowledging mistakes. Therefore, it is crucial to assess what we own and consider the opportunity cost associated with that ownership.

10.   Target Bias

Some market participants adopt a mindset of *"I want to achieve X amount of return (the 'target')"* and plan to sell and exit once they reach that goal. However, this psychology-driven focus on price movement may not yield benefits in the long term.

If a business deteriorates, the declining stock price may not reach the target price. As a result, capital becomes tied up in a poorly performing business, leading to lost opportunities elsewhere, known as *opportunity cost*.

Conversely, suppose the target price is achieved, and shares are sold. In that case, investors may miss out on the potential long-term growth of *a wonderful business that continues to compound invested capital year after year.* By selling, we break that powerful chain of growth.

It is essential to make rational decisions based on a solid investment framework. Avoid emotional stock-trading decisions that could jeopardize your profit-making opportunities over time, particularly by preventing panic selling.

2.2   Cultivate the Right Mindset

Cultivating the right mindset is crucial to achieving success in the stock market. This is the golden rule. It will help you to play the investment game effectively and stay in the game. It is most important aspect in the investment.

Selling should be your ultimate option. It is crucial to recognize the mistakes of either selling a compounding business too early or holding (not selling) onto a mediocre business, which can dampen your overall performance in the stock market.

Seller's emotions play a central role in mistakes within the stock market. Here are some common emotional pitfalls:

- ***Greed*** can lead to two types of mistakes: a) Selling a wonderful business too quickly to pocket immediate profits. b) Holding onto a mediocre stock in the hope that its price will rises.

- ***Fear*** can drive investors to: a) Sell a wonderful business to cut perceived losses. b) Hold onto a mediocre business while waiting for price recovery.

- ***Envy*** creates anxiety about missing out if you do not buy and sell during a rising stock market.

- ***Regret*** inevitably grips stock market participants' sooner or later. This negative emotion can create discomfort and may turn the investment journey into a distressing experience.

These emotions can easily and unconsciously impair our rational decision-making abilities, leading to mistakes.

To address the issue, I dedicated an entire section – 'Self Mastery' of my previous book, **'The Intelligent Investor's Approach to Risk Mastery'**.

I believe it was the first holistic investment risk management book.

Conversely, once stocks are sold, emotions can take on a different dynamic:

- If the stock price declines further after sell, we may feel validated, believing we made the right decision.

- If the stock price rises after selling, we often regret missing out on those profits.

- If the stock prices remain stagnant, for some time, our mind starts playing tricks on us. Either – a) fostering expectations for a future price increase, or b) creating a sense of having missed an opportunity to sell and invest in other rising stocks.

*Little more about '**Regret**' as it is one of the most commonly and widely felt emotion in the stock market.*

Regret feeling is often triggered when a stock price increases after selling, not buying, or purchasing only a minimal number of shares. It is not uncommon to sell a stock only to see its price climb afterward, leading to feelings of missed profit opportunities. Overcoming this state of mind is essential for maintaining a healthy investment outlook.

The right mindset stems from a well-defined investment framework. As intelligent investors, it is crucial to establish strategies that align with your Conviction, Courage, and Comfort. This alignment is key to compounding your wealth.

Your selling decision should be rooted in a well-defined investment framework, making it a strategic choice rather than an emotional reaction. Therefore, it is unproductive to feel regret if the price rises after your sale; this does not imply that your reasoning for buying and holding was flawed.

Remember, the stock price is not obligated to decline after you sell. The market often requires time to recognize deteriorating business prospects. Instead of dwelling on past decisions, focus on identifying the next promising opportunity that could lead to long-term compounding growth.

*****

3 Master *Why* Behind Every Sell

"If you are not aggressive, you are not going to make money, and if you are not defensive, you are not going to keep money."

— Ray Dalio

To successfully navigate your investment journey, it is essential to cultivate the right perspective and mindset toward selling. This mindset should be clearly articulated in your written framework and strategies.

> *One crucial point to recognize and accept is that whenever the idea of 'selling' arises, it often aligns more with trading or speculation rather than true investing.*

Let me emphasize again: *buying with intention to sell is either trading or speculation.*

There is nothing inherently wrong with trading or speculation, but approaching these activities with the right mindset and perspective is crucial for effective strategy development.

The 'cigar-butt' investing termed by Warren Buffett is also one type of trading. It made him to reap the gains and multiple the capital in the early days of investment journey.

Investing should be approached as if you are running a business – embracing an ownership mindset.

With this perspective, you begin to think and behave differently. It is essential to master the following principles:

> ***Selling is riskier than buying; those who understand it build lasting wealth in the stock market.***

If we take a moment to reflect, we realize that traders and speculators focus on price fluctuations to execute their buy and sell decisions.

Your 'why' for selling lies at the heart of the selling process. Understanding it prompts you to consider the significance *of selling*.

Two crucial parameters influence a stock's price:

1. The underlying company's prospects

2. The prevailing sentiment in the market

Before we delve into *why to sell*, we must recognize and understand *our **Role – Identity** in the market.*

3.2 Your Role - Your Market Edge

In the stock market, participants generally fall into three categories - roles: *trader, speculator, and investor.*

Understanding *"who am I?"* is vital, as it helps establish our identity and approach the market appropriately to execute our roles successfully.

Player 1: **The Trader**

A trader identifies gaps between price and value when deciding to buy or sell. They estimate this gap using a desirable Margin of Safety (MoS). This discrepancy may arise from the market's ignorance of a company's true value or changes in the company's prospects. Such changes can result from various factors, including expansion, mergers and acquisitions, shifts in management, or the discovery of new economic assets like patents or valuable resources such as oil and gas.

The legendary investor Warren Buffett famously referred to this strategy as 'cigar-butt' investing,' a concept he utilized extensively in his early career to grow capital for himself and his partners before being influenced by Charlie Munger to adopt a different approach.

Player 2: **The Speculator**

In contrast, a speculator acts based on observable patterns or statistical indicators and tends to overlook the underlying business fundamentals. Instead, they focus on price momentum, hoping to profit from market transactions. Speculation knows no bounds in terms of potential risk or reward.

Player 3: **The Investor**

An investor approaches the market with a business-like mindset. Their primary focus is on the company's ability to generate shareholder value. The investor is concerned with growth prospects and dividend payments as a business owner.

Investors thoroughly analyze the underlying company, aiming to identify its economic prospects in relation to its current market price. Considerations of value and growth inform decisions.

Each market participant operates to aim for future benefits unfolding uncertainties—risk. These variables can significantly influence outcomes, either positively or negatively.

This raises a crucial question: What are the characteristics of each participant in the game?

Each participant navigates distinct zones characterized by genre, risk tolerance, timeframe, and mindset.

Understanding your role and your zone of interest is essential. It allows you to perceive reality differently, minimizing mistakes and regrets.

Decisions in transactions should align with your role—whether you are a trader, speculator, or investor. While it is possible for one individual to assume multiple roles, it is vital to understand the characteristics associated with each zone to avoid confusion and errors.

Ideally, an investor should view their stock holdings as a business owner, perpetually holding onto company shares. However, in a dynamic environment filled with opportunities, it is essential to weigh the risk-reward ratio rationally. Thus, selling decisions should be informed by the company's prospects and the opportunity cost.

A trader purchases a stock to sell it later. They enter the trade knowing the specific reasons behind the gap between the stock's price and its intrinsic value. Once the gap disappears, it is time for the trader to sell.

In contrast, a speculator primarily focuses on selling for profit, relying on heuristics—rules of thumb that may or may not be valid for a given situation or timeframe. They aim to make money by the end of the trading day and seek quick exits.

All participants must recognize that selling is essential to complete the transaction cycle. The difference lies in their perspective on the stock market, which influences their time horizons. The outcome can vary widely, resulting in either profits or losses, potentially making participants wealthy or leading them to bankruptcy.

It is essential to understand your role in the market—whether as a trader, speculator, or investor—and to act accordingly. I recommend that you:

1. Clearly define your role in a transaction.

2. Establish a specific zone within a well-designed framework for buying, selling, or holding assets.

3.3 The Importance of Selling

Every market participant will eventually need to sell, depending on their role. Selling is crucial because it is the only way to realize profits or losses. Until a stock is sold, your capital remains tied up in the market.

The value of your investment fluctuates with market sentiment on any given day. You may see variations in your portfolio as profits or losses based on the difference between your purchase price and the current stock price. However, these are merely numbers on the screen. Only after selling the stock can you realize your financial outcome, whether a profit or a loss.

A trader or speculator sells with the primary goal of profiting from the transaction. In contrast, an investor sells to reallocate capital into a more promising opportunity, rectify a previous buying mistake, or respond to deteriorating business prospects.

Regardless of your role in the market, it is crucial to define your own rules for selling and adhere to them diligently to avoid future regrets. We will explore these rules in the upcoming chapters.

*****

A Bit of My Experience:

Over the past two decades in the stock market, I have primarily occupied two roles:

1. **Trader:** I bought stocks intending to sell them later, driven by corporate events, noticeable gaps in price and value, or turnaround stories. My selling strategy focused on the convergence of price towards its intrinsic value. In the early days, I might not have fully understood every business, but the gap between price and value was always clear. My time frame for holding stocks was typically a few months to a couple of years, and my decision to sell was always well thought out in advance.

    The idea behind trading was to generate capital for purchasing a stake in a business as an investor, allowing the compounding machine to operate over time.

2. **Investor:** As an investor, I focused on thoroughly understanding the businesses I invested in. I placed great importance on my comfort level with the management team,

ensuring they were trustworthy and capable of driving effective growth for the company.

I sold my investments primarily for two reasons:

a) Need for Funds: There were times when I required cash and had no other options available. In hindsight, this was often a mistake, as it interrupted the compounding process. A big mistake!

b) Deteriorating Business Signals: I sold when there were clear indicators that the business was losing its potential.

I will discuss additional rules and reasons for selling in subsequent chapters. My focus as an investor is build enduring wealth and achieving financial freedom, aiming for sure-fire multi-baggers over time. I had the patience and conviction to hold onto these investments.

I suggest you clearly define your *'why'* for selling to build your wealth-generating autopilot machine.

*****

3.4 Why Selling is Harder and Riskier?

Our emotions compound the complexities of the stock market, and selling is no exception. The key to effective selling is straightforward: ***if you buy a stock or a business for a good reason, you should sell it for an even better reason.***

Otherwise, selling loses its rationale. Regardless of short-term market price volatility, you should not be overly concerned. Adopting this mindset allows you to be critical when buying but demands even greater scrutiny and rationality when selling. Thus, selling requires more conviction and discipline than buying.

Selling becomes challenging and riskier when the seller is unclear about why they purchased the stock in the first place or what role they are playing in the market. In such a scenario, the individual often resorts to speculative behavior, relying on the sentiments and opinions of other market participants.

You never know if a stock you own could become a multi-bagger after selling it. The potential for upward movement can be significant, and by selling, you might miss out on substantial gains.

Conversely, if a stock's price drops to zero, your loss is limited to the capital you initially invested. This highlights that mistakes in selling can be riskier than those made in buying.

Let's remind ourselves -

> ***Selling is riskier than buying; those who understand it build lasting wealth in the stock market.***

*****

4 Master The Right Sell Time – *When?*

"If you get on the wrong train and immediately realize it, get off at the next nearest station.
The longer it takes you to get off, the more expensive the return trip will be."

– Japanese Proverb

Selling can be tricky. When you are wrong, you risk losing your entire capital allocation. However, when you are right, you can reap the rewards of compounding.

You will typically find yourself selling in one of two scenarios:

- **Proactive Approach:** This involves selling with a clear plan, defined goals, and control based on your investment framework. You might sell when the price converges with the underlying value, when prices reach euphoric levels due to opportunity costs, the need for funds, or to correct a buying mistake.

- **Reactive Approach:** This involves unplanned selling driven by emotions, sentiments, regrets, or irrational behavior. You might find yourself selling due to falling crowds, a lack of edge, or in the context of speculation.

Reactive selling typically lacks a strategic framework. The risks are highest in these impulsive reactions, as they are often based solely on price movements rather than a well-considered plan.

Establishing clear selling rules and strategies is essential for effectively selling. This proactive mindset helps avoid emotional biases and minimizes mistakes and regrets.

4.1 Revisiting the Initial Purchase Decision

An intelligent investor operates within a well-defined framework and strategy in the stock market. A critical aspect of this approach is clearly understanding **why** they purchased a particular stock. This rationale could be based on business fundamentals, management quality, or a compelling price-value gap.

Determining why to sell becomes straightforward when your reasons for buying are well-articulated. Any deviations from these foundational reasons – especially if they undermine the business's prospects – should signal a clear sell decision.

Define your reasons for buying clearly to cultivate a more proactive selling strategy. This clarity will simplify the process of holding and selling in the future.

4.2 Strategic Selling

The first rule to is to avoid selling under pressure. You sell only based on facts that you predefined. Invest in companies poised for long-term growth, allowing you to leverage the power of compounding rather than feeling compelled to sell in response to a declining stock price.

Stock sales can be planned strategically. While this approach may not always guarantee success, it can help you adhere to key principles and avoid being swayed by short-term price fluctuations.

Over the past two decades, I divided my stock portfolio into two categories: **a) Trading** and **b) Investments.** Trading stocks was based on identifying price-to-value gaps and generating cash for reinvestment. Importantly, I never bought shares with borrowed money;

I created capital through trading. Although this process took longer, it provided peace of mind and a sense of security.

The cash generated from selling in the trading category was split, typically 50- 50. The first 50% went toward additional trades, often employing a 'cigar-butt' investment approach—targeting undervalued stocks for potential short-term gains. The remaining 50% was invested in long-term compounding business models—companies with the durability to build wealth and provide financial freedom over time.

In this process, I achieved several multi-baggers – some yielding returns from 3x to as much as 60x. These gains allowed me to build a solid fund base, which I then directed toward long-term, compounding businesses. This highlights that ***when approached strategically, sales can be powerful tools for generating cash and*** creating wealth.

4.3 Key Questions Before Selling

Consider asking yourself key questions to maintain rationality and avoid emotional traps when selling. Keep a journal for your reasoning. It will help you rationalize the selling process and build your investment framework and strategies. Journals provide valuable insights and help in generating new ideas in the future.

If a sell decision proves correct, it clarifies why and how your judgment worked. Conversely, if the sell results in a mistake – like a forced premature exit or an unwise buy – you gain a chance to refine your strategy and improve future decisions.

1. Why did I buy?

2. Why do I want to sell now?

3. Is this stock intended for trading or long-term investment?

4. Did my original investment thesis fail?

5. Do I have a better opportunity to deploy funds?

6. Am I emotionally inclined to sell due to personal mood or market sentiments?

7. How would I feel if sell now, but the business performed well and the stock became multi-bagger over time?

8. Is a full exit necessary, or would trimming the position suffice?

9. What if I did not sell, even if the price dropped to 40-50% from the buy price?

*****

5 Rules for Selling as an Investor

"The first rule of compounding: Never interrupt it unnecessarily."

— Charlie Munger

An investor approaches stock with an ownership mindset. The stock represents interest in part of the business. The ownership mindset has the following characteristics and benefits:

1. Discipline in evaluating the business thoroughly before owning the stock of the company.

2. Commitment to hold the stock as long as the buy thesis is intact.

3. Be party to the business value creation and growth.

4. At regular interval evaluation of management decisions, business

economics and overall industry scenario.

5. Allow invested capital to compound over time.

6. Accumulate the dividends (if any) to reinvest in the business or in any other opportunities.

7. Provides greater financial stability and peace of mind.

8. Presents the opportunity to participate in corporate actions actively.

In an ideal scenario, an investor would never sell the shares in a business that continues to perform well.

However, the stock market offers the *flexibility to sell* stock at any time, which, while advantageous, is a double-edged sword. You must exercise this option wisely in making effective sell-or-hold decisions to avoid mediocre performance.

As an investor with an ownership mindset, you should keep shares as long as the business grows satisfactorily. This will reward you with dividends and capital appreciation over time. Yet, in a rapidly evolving world marked by disruptions, intense competition, and changing customer and market demands, even a well-performing business may face obstacles to growth or survival.

Therefore, it is essential to establish a clear framework for selling, either when identifying permanent issues within the company or discovering an exceptional new opportunity aligned with a significant market trend.

The following *guiding rules help an investor determine why and when to sell.*

As an intelligent investor, you should identify your business portfolios' losers and winners. Losers should be considered for *sell based on their value and growth prospects, risk-reward balance, or opportunity cost.*

Let us explore the rules for selling as an intelligent investor with ownership mindset.

Rule No. 1:

Sell When You Discover the Buy Was a Mistake.

"It ain't what you don't know that gets you into trouble. It's what you know for sure that just ain't so."

– Mark Twain

As an investor, you study and investigate the facts about the company, management, and business environment before deciding to buy shares. The process is guided by your investment framework. However, later, you may discover additional facts detrimental to the company's prospects. Even after thorough analysis, it is possible to miss certain elements related to the business model, management, or competition that could ultimately harm the company's economy.

When this happens, it is time to correct the mistake. Correcting errors early is preferable. Avoid emotional attachment to the company – even if you spent considerable time researching it. Use unbiased judgment and sell unemotionally. Falling in love with a stock is *an easy trap* could be avoided with disciplined decision-making process.

<u>Rule No. 2</u>:

Sell Losers Sooner Rather Than Later.

This rule is supplementary to Rule No.1. It is human psychology to hold on to losing stock for two main reasons:

1) **Loss Aversion Bias:** This bias can prevent you from selling and taking losses. As the pain of losing money feels more significant than the pleasure of gaining an equivalent amount.

2) **Perceived Value:** Lower stock prices can create the illusion of being 'cheap,' leading an investor to average down on their losses in hopes that a turnaround is just around the corner.

Holding onto losing stock is a mistake that consumes your mental resources and keeps you from investing that capital in better opportunities.

Taking prompt action to sell can help you:

1. **Minimize Losses:** Selling sooner can prevent further declines that negatively impact your overall performance.

2. **Free Up Capital:** You can reallocate your funds to more promising investments by selling.

3. **Clear Your Mind:** Letting go of underperforming stocks allows you to focus your mental energy on more valuable opportunities.

Intentionally Left Blank

Rule No. 3:

Sell When There Is Permanent Deterioration in Business Economics.

You may have purchased a company's stock when the business performed well and its prospects appeared promising. However, over time, you might discover that the financials are not improving as expected. This could be due to a failure in the business model or irreparable operational issues.

If you notice a consistent decline in prospects, it is crucial to take action. Once you recognize that the business financials are not improving, you can sell the stock immediately. Alternatively, you could strategize to sell gradually your position if the price rises.

A prudent approach is to recover your invested capital and consider taking profits in stages.

However, if you are facing losses, it is generally better to sell sooner rather than later to mitigate further damage to your portfolio.

Rule No. 4:

Sell When There is Evidence or a Pattern of Suspicious Accounting or Fraudulent Activities.

As an intelligent and active investor, cultivating a habit of thorough investigation is essential to detect accounting fraud early. Annual reports and financial statements contain many warning signs.

For example, companies may try to disguise high debt as investments; in such cases, examine cash flows to determine if these so-called 'investments' provide any financial benefits.

Other red flags include overstating revenue or profits, understating expenses, inflating asset values, manipulating inventory levels, and so forth.

These signals are often hidden within details in annual reports, financial statements, and footnotes.

Additional warning signs may include frequent resignations of auditors or independent directors or sudden changes in accounting practices.

By identifying these red flags promptly, at first place, you can restrain from buying such company stocks. If you realized after buying you could sell and exit well in advance before the frauds been reported. It will potentially protect your portfolio from significant losses.

Intentionally Left Blank

Rule No. 5:

Sell When Industry Disruption Occurs and the Company Fails to Adapt.

Innovations in science and technology create significant disruptions that can challenge a company's market position or even threaten its existence. As a long-term investor, monitoring a company's agility and ability to respond to shifting market conditions is essential.

For instance, a breakthrough molecule may offer effective and affordable treatment options in pharmaceutical sectors, reshaping the competitive landscape.

Innovations in operational processes can enhance productivity and efficiency, while disruptive products can change how consumers engage with goods and services.

For instance, new-generation mobile phones have revolutionized consumer expectations by combining communication, entertainment, and camera functions into one device.

These shifts can erode a company's '*moat*' – its sustainable competitive advantage. If a business fails to recognize and adapt to such disruptions, it risks obsolescence. Companies like Nokia, BlackBerry, and Kodak have served as cautionary examples. They once were industry leaders in their respective marketplace. But ultimately could not keep pace with innovation and fell from their glorious past.

As an investor, you play a crucial role in recognizing changes in industry and market dynamics. This awareness empowers you to plan your selling strategy, whether in a single transaction or gradually based on unfolding scenarios.

Intentionally Left Blank

Rule No. 6:

Sell When the Company Faces Frequent or Persistent Labor Issues.

Industries are prone to labor issues, such as workers' compensation, morale, or retention. These problems can undermine company culture and productivity. They might be inherent in businesses due to their labor-intensive operations. These industries face consistent pressure from rising labor costs, unequal trade policies, or competition from low-cost markets worldwide.

Signs of labor unrest are often reflected in decreased business efficiency, financial reporting weaknesses, and strained financial ratios. These challenges are particularly pronounced in commodity businesses, where costs are sensitive to inflation and operational disruptions. Ideally, it is best to avoid investing in these types of companies. If already invested, it is wise to recognize these warning signs and sell before issues become more entrenched.

<u>Rule No. 7</u>:

Sell When Facing a Legal Tussle That Could Make the Business Unsustainable.

A company may encounter legal issues related to its brand or trademark, challenging its ownership of goodwill and popularity. Other legal concerns may include intellectual property, contractual, licensing, land disputes, or business ownership (promoters).

By analysing the financial reports from the past few years, you can identify the escalation of various cost factors and understand that potential doom might be imminent. At this point, it is prudent to consider selling your shares.

Rule No. 8:

Sell When Management Exhibits Undesirable Behavior Toward the Business or Shareholders.

Management should lead the business toward sustainable growth, allocating capital effectively to maximize shareholder value. This could be done by expanding the current business, creating new revenue streams, or strengthening the company's competitive moat.

If you observe that management consistently falls short of expectations or engages in unethical practices, it is a clear warning of challenging times ahead. These issues may not be immediately reflected in financial reports, but as a long-term investor, you should be observant.

Indicators of declining management quality could include weak business growth, poor capital allocation, or decisions that stray from the company's core values.

Your disagreements with recent strategic directions, especially those involving shortcuts or ethical compromises, are red flags.

Another concerning pattern is management behavior that prioritizes short-term stock price manoeuvres – such as selling shares when the price is high and repurchasing when it drops – over the business's long-term health. Actions like these suggest focusing on market manipulation rather than business fundamentals, signalling it may be time to exit your investment.

It is well said that, - "You cannot expect a good deal from a bad person."

Intentionally Left Blank

<u>Rule No. 9:</u>

Sell When Management Starts Playing Adventurous Games That Harm Business Economics.

Management may engage in mergers and acquisitions (M&As) to force synergy or drive top-line growth.

Management takes pride in these activities as give media coverages and keep them engaged. However, poorly considered mergers can harm the business's financial health. Many M&As are short-lived ventures that ultimately add little value and, in some cases, become financial burdens.

If this pattern becomes evident, it may be time to sell and exit the investment.

<u>Rule No. 10</u>:

Sell When You Observe Suspicious or Unusual Insider Selling Activities.

When members of the broader management or promoters begin selling large amounts of company stock, it can be a red flag.

Occasional sales for personal financial needs are understandable, but frequent, widespread insider selling warrants closer scrutiny.

Such patterns may indicate emerging issues within the company, hinting at potential challenges to future growth or stability. By investigating these activities early, you can make a timely decision to sell and protect your investment.

Rule No. 11:

Sell to Redeploy the Capital into an Exceptionally Better Opportunity.

> *"Everything is a function of opportunity cost."*
>
> — Warren Buffett

Capital is always limited, though its size can vary. If an exceptional opportunity arises, and you lack the capital to invest, selling some of your current holdings may be the only option.

To make this decision, evaluate it against the ***principle of opportunity cost***: *the new investment must be significantly superior to the business you are considering selling.* The opportunity cost should be high enough to justify replacing your current holding with this new prospect.

When making this decision, it is crucial to assess it carefully. Compare the potential business prospects, advantages from major market trends, and the growth clarity offered by the new opportunity's expansion plans or project realizations. This careful assessment will give you conviction and confidence in your investment decisions.

In this context, it is not about chasing returns; it's about your analysis and expectation that the new opportunity is significantly better than the one you currently hold. If that is the case, freeing up capital for the more promising investment makes sense.

This emphasis on the new opportunity being significantly better will make you feel confident in your decision-making.

Intentionally Left Blank

Rule No. 12:

Sell to Rebalance the Business Portfolio... *With Caution.*

This decision depends on your risk appetite and investment framework, particularly regarding maximum exposure to a single company. If your position in a stock exceeds your comfort level or constitutes a substantial portion of your portfolio, you might consider selling a portion to rebalance.

This choice can be complex. Even if business fundamentals remain unchanged, holding an outsized position may create emotional discomfort, prompting you to reduce your stake.

Alternatively, you might set limits on maximum capital allocation or concentration within your portfolio as a structured approach to rebalancing.

The rebalancing is a double-sward. It could also be possible that the out-paced company has potential to compound future. As cautious approach is the key in either selling or holding.

Rule No. 13:

Sell a Growth Stock and Switch to a Dividend Stock.

As an investor, you may have initially purchased a stock in a growth industry. However, over time, obstacles to growth – such as technological disruptions, industry saturation, or company-specific issues – can make further expansion challenging.

Suppose you are now in a later stage of life and prioritizing financial stability. In that case, it may be worth selling this growth stock and redeploying the capital into high dividend-paying ones.

Dividend stocks, typically from large corporations, often offer stable cash flows that align with a shift toward income-focused financial goals.

This approach allows you to focus on growth during your younger years and then gradually transition to dividend investments as you aim for more steady and continuous income in the future.

Rule No. 14:

Sell if Regular Dividends Are Eliminated or in a Reducing Trend.

As an investor, you can earn through stock price appreciation (capital gain) only when you sell the stock or through dividends.

A strong business grows over time and increases profits, reflected in stock price appreciation. Additionally, the company may reward shareholders through dividends, which indicates the business's stability and growth. If a company stops paying dividends or reduces the rate without clear reinvestment, this can be a red flag.

A dividend cut is a serious event, potentially signaling financial challenges or changes that investors should monitor closely.

Dividend investing focuses on stocks that pay dividends and offer a steady income source. *Remember, paying dividend to shareholders is sigh of real cash the business is generating.*

While companies are not obligated to pay dividends, a reduction may not always imply financial trouble—it could reflect a strategic choice to reinvest in growth, retain earnings, or fund research and development.

Dividend cuts are not always negative; however, if your primary goal in investment is to generate income through steady stream of dividends then, it might be the right time to sell the stock.

Intentionally Left Blank

Rule No. 15:

Do Not Sell Based on Price Action or an Increase in the Stock Price.

Do not sell solely based on the increase in the stock price (market valuation).

Mediocre market participants often chase returns, buying what has performed well in the past and selling what has fallen in price. These actions are driven solely by price movements and typically generate mediocre returns. A sign of speculation.

The issue also affects many mutual funds. In their pursuit of returns and to meet fund flow requirements, they often follow the crowd mentality, buying at the top and selling at the bottom.

Instead, focus on making informed buy and sell decisions.

As long as the underline business is growing and adding value the increase in stock price should not bother an investor. Selling in such cases is mistake, as compounding gets interrupted. Hence a lifetime opportunity to accumulate the wealth.

Rule No. 16:

Sell When You Need Money to Address Emergency Situation... *as a Last Resort.*

In the stock market, you may be conditioned to sell a performing business stock at the wrong time due to an urgent need for money.

This bad timing often stems from inadequate financial planning, highlighting the importance of preparing to fund emergencies without selling when the market does not value your holdings.

You may need cash to meet urgent needs for yourself and your family, particularly when financial planning is lacking. *In such situations, it is advisable to take a calculated approach to selling a stock with limited growth prospects and sell only a portion of the shares as required.*

Being forced to sell in distress can lead to a profitable or loss-making transaction, but it is generally unsafe. Thus, I always emphasize the importance of maintaining cash in your financial planning to handle daily needs and emergencies. This preparation is crucial for navigating real-life crises.

Also, there could be a real crisis in financial markets. Therefore, maintaining a cash position is an active choice within your investment framework. The optimum level may range from 5% to 50%, depending on the opportunity cost you observe in the market. This should be as high as possible to justify entering a promising business for long-term compounding.

In summary, it is essential to have an emergency fund readily available at all times. Consequently, effective financial planning is fundamental to a successful investment journey.

*****

6 Rules for Selling as a Trader

"If you use less emotion in investing, in trading, don't use any emotion. It has to be emotionless."

– Rakesh Jhunjhunwala

A trader looks at gaps between stock price and value based on underlying assets and cash flows. They may arise from a business turnaround, mergers and acquisitions, business spin-offs, changes in management, market sentiment, or asset base valuation. These represent trading opportunities—a value gap. They ***may not be*** suitable for long-term compounding. Typically, they are short-term to mid-term strategies to generate profit and build your capital base. A trader invests based on a price-value gap. Professor Benjamin Graham calls this gap the '*Margin of Safety' (MoS)*, while Warren Buffett calls it *'cigar-butt investing.' In this approach, a trader adopts a value-investing mindset but with selling in mind.*

The major issue is that you must find consistent opportunities in the market where the odds are in your favor. There is a danger that you mistake a *false* event for a chance, OR the convergence of value and price could take an extended period, impacting your opportunity cost.

Hence, traders are exposed to higher risk. One significant risk traders face is their own emotions and biases. A trader must be right twice—once when buying and once when selling. Consequently, with more transactions involved compared to an investor, traders face greater risks.

While an investor buys a piece of business to hold perpetually. Sell is only considered for reasons as discussed in the previous chapter.

The trader's job is to monitor its performance and keep the opportunity cost at the highest levels before considering a switch to a better opportunity.

Selling is trickier and harder for a trader because it involves identifying the price and value gap. Have patience to wait for the cost to converge with the business value. Selling is also more tactical. Therefore, it is essential to make the effective selling decisions based on your predefined framework and selling rules.

To become a successful trader, you must demonstrate patience, discipline, and objectivity in making successful sell decisions.

The following are golden selling rules for *traders (not speculators)*. You can incorporate or modify them based on your investment framework, strategies, risk appetite, and opportunity cost (risk-reward ratio).

<u>Rule No. 1:</u>

Sell When the Stock Price Converges to the Intrinsic Value of the Business.

A value investor with a trading mindset buys when he identifies a price gap between the market and a business's intrinsic value. This intrinsic value is determined by the business's capacity for cash flow generation, discounted at a fair rate in relation to government-secured bonds or treasury bills.

Another valuation method considers the business's assets, such as land and properties, valued based on current market prices. In this scenario, the stock market may not accurately reflect the company's value, especially if growth is limited. Consequently, the price might take long to align with the intrinsic value. Prof. Benjamin Graham referred to this as a *'liquidation value.'*

You should sell the stock when its price converges to valuation levels. However, if the business demonstrates growth potential and the prospect of increased profits, you may choose to hold the stock longer before selling.

<u>Rule No. 2:</u>

Sell When the Stock Prices Rise Too High in Comparison to Underlying Business Value.

OR

Sell When the Market is in a Bubble Phase.

This rule supplements Rule #1. You may keep holding as a value investor based on the business's growth potential and future cash flows.

However, if *the stock price rises to a euphoric level* – perhaps due to excessive optimism about the company, industry, in a bull market, media hype, or widespread positive sentiment about the economy – it may be time to sell. When too much optimism is factored into the price, selling can be prudent.

As a trader, you benefit from holding the stock for growth potential, but market euphoria may prompt you to sell early as the price surges.

You can identify bubble situations in the following cases:

a) The Price-to-Earnings (P/E) ratio is too high to justify the near or mid-term.

b) Media and broker reports are overwhelmingly bullish.

c) A flood of new Initial Public Offerings (IPOs) is hitting the primary market.

d) High prices overlook any potential negative events or challenges.

In such cases, no one can predict exactly when a bull run will end, or a bubble might burst. Therefore, you should plan your selling strategy carefully.

Selling in stages rather than all at once can be advantageous. To secure a profitable trade, consider first selling enough shares to *recover your purchase cost*; any additional gains will then represent *pure profit*.

In trading, recouping the purchase cost early can provide peace of mind, making you feel more comfortable while experiencing high stock prices in a bull market.

The freed-up capital can then be redirected toward long-term investments, traded in opportunities where a significant price-value gap exists, or temporarily parked in liquid funds, ready to be deployed into future trades or investments.

Rule No. 3:

Sell When an Anticipated Corporate Event Gets Materialized and the Stock Price Adjusted Accordingly.

A company is treated as *a separate entity* from its owners and based on *ongoing* principles. Hence, it is perpetual as long as it is formally terminated. A company's lifecycle goes through multiple events, such as market expansions, new business verticals, mergers and acquisitions, or spin-offs.

These events change the valuation game. Based on facts and insights, you could be a first mover. Once the market recognizes the value of the event, the stock is re-rated to a higher price based on possible value creation.

This is the time to sell if the underlying business is mediocre and you see little future growth prospects. It is most likely a one-time event. Even if it grows in the future, it may not bring considerable value appreciation.

These are the opportunities to rerate the business value. In such cases, you could take advantage of the first mover to buy the stock at lower levels.

And once the event materialized and stock price increase to intrinsic value then you could get the opportunity to sell.

On the contrary, there could be a negative corporate event in the company where you hold the stock.

The event could be:

  a. The company could diversify into unrelated business segments where management lacks experience and expertise. It is a high-risk event.

  b. When the company has been acquired and you are uncomfortable with new management.

  c. Any misfortunate event like fire or loss of key management personnel.

These negatively affecting events must be scrutinized, and decisions must be made on whether to hold or sell.

Rule No. 4:

Sell Based on Specific Corporate Actions.

Many companies announce corporate actions like stock splits or bonus issues to attract shareholders, often generating positive sentiment and potentially pushing the stock price higher.

You can take advantage of the momentum by playing the *'buy low, sell high'* game or using the *opportunity to correct any buy mistakes.*

Note: These actions do not change the underlying value of the business. Hence a favorable price action is an opportunity for you to sell.

Rule No. 5:

Follow the Private Equity Formula to Sell.

Private Equity (PE) firms often buy struggling companies, injecting capital and improving management to turn them around for a higher resale value.

In some cases, PE firms invest in skilled management to build and grow the business and eventually take it public.

The strategy is clear: increase the company's value—short or long-term—and exit by selling the shares.

We must acknowledge that these PE funds have obligations towards their unit holders (shareholders) to generate consistent profits.

By monitoring these PE actions within a company, you can gauge the right times to buy or sell based on disciplined exit principles. This approach offers a model to follow, helping you make more informed trading decisions.

Rule No. 6:

Sell When Growth Stocks Stop Growing.

A company's growth typically comes from launching new products and services, expanding into new geographical markets, or introducing product variations – all of which boost revenue, profits, and, in turn, stock valuation.

However, over time, various factors, such as increased competition, shifts in market demand, and the emergence of new or more affordable products, can limit or stall growth.

When these opposing forces limit the company's growth, it is likely time to sell. As the reasons for buying the stock in the company's expansion no longer hold.

<u>Rule No. 7</u>:

Sell Once the Stock Reaches Your Predefined Target Price.

In trading, you might buy stocks to sell later for various reasons based on your strategies - sell rules. You must hold sell option at your own discretion.

One common strategy is to set a predefined target price, such as a 10% or 20% increase, at which you plan to sell. However, it is important to recognize that this approach *leans more toward speculation*, where you purchase a stock with the hope of selling it at a higher price based on your target.

Engaging in this strategy can be riskier, and I do not recommend making it a frequent practice unless you have a favorable assessment of the odds. Since it is speculative, there is a possibility that you might incur losses or that it could take a significant amount of time to reach the target price.

Selling is an art. You can effectively combine your strategy with anticipated corporate events or actions. This blend allows you to capitalize on market movements and make informed decisions while navigating the complexities of trading.

Intentionally Left Blank

<u>Rule No. 8</u>:

Sell When the Stock Price is Clearly in a Downtrend.

In this case, selling is a *trend-pattern* strategy. The downward price pattern occurs when a company does not show signs of a turnaround or takes a long time to generate cash. This may be due to its obligations—liabilities and loans—while business performance deteriorates.

A potential business turnaround often lacks solid backing - evidence in the stock's downtrend.

In such situations, selling and exiting sooner is a wiser option than averaging down by purchasing more shares at lower prices. This approach allows you to preserve capital and avoid further losses while seeking better investment opportunities.

Rule No. 9:

Sell When the Stock Price Has Stagnated for a Long Time.

There could be multiple reasons for a stock price to remain stagnant:

1. **Lack of Improvement:** You may have purchased shares based on expectations of a turnaround or a change in management that would enhance the business's value. However, if there are no noticeable improvements in the financial metrics, this may signal trouble.

2. **Mediocre Performance:** The business may be performing mediocrely, with management lacking ambition for growth. There may be high competition or operating maximum factory capacity, and no plans to expand the capacities.

   If growth is not evident and no proactive measures are taken, selling and investing in a company with better opportunities might be wise.

3. **Market Sentiment:** Conversely, stock price stagnation could occur

because larger market participants have not recognized the business's value, or general market sentiment may be bearish. In his case, patience is key; however, if you sense that the stagnation will persist, selling may be prudent.

4. **Trading Volume:** One more aspect traders need to consider is trading volume. The stock price remains in a narrow band with low trading volume—essentially stagnating. The lower the volume for such a stock, the more challenging it becomes to sell, even when you know the company is on a downward trajectory.

   The playing game in this scenario can be tricky and challenging. Your best option is to sell at every opportunity when buyers emerge, as waiting for a more favorable moment may lead to further losses.

Intentionally Left Blank

Rule No. 10:

Sell When There is a Change in the Industry Economic Cycle in Which the Company Operates.

As a trader, you aim to pocket profits swiftly, which allows you to rotate capital towards promising newer opportunities.

When an industry's cycle turns down—specifically in commodity-type businesses—it becomes challenging for companies to achieve above-average profits and margins, as they compete mainly on price points.

Hence, if you are trading in a commodity company, then keeping watch on cycles and trends is essential to deciding whether to buy or sell.

*The following **sell rules** pertain to what **you should avoid doing**:*

Rule No. 11:

Do Not Sell in a Hurry.

It goes back to our earlier lessons about why we purchased the stock. If the reasoning for your buy decision fails, it makes sense to sell immediately.

However, do not rush into selling. If your buy thesis remains intact, but the stock price is dropping or stagnating, critically recheck the facts to decide whether to continue holding or selling.

Market sentiment can swing prices in either direction. So avoid hasty decisions. Conduct your independent analysis and make a sound judgment before selling.

<u>Rule No. 12</u>:

Do Not Sell All of Your Holdings in a New Industry Opportunity – *A Megatrend.*

In trading, once prices meet your target, consider selling some of your holdings to recover your investment cost. If you have achieved a good profit in the stock,
selling a percentage of your holdings might be considered while allowing the remainder to continue growing.

This strategy offers several advantages:

1. **Cost Recovery:** You recoup your initial investment by selling a portion, reducing your risk exposure.

2. **Realized Profit:** You secure some profit in your account, providing a buffer against potential losses in the future. As initial euphoria could lift prices too high to justify the near future growth potential.

3. **Compounding Growth:** Keeping a portion of your holdings allows you to benefit from potential future growth, especially in emerging industries that are megatrends.

Such situations often arise in new and promising industries where initial euphoria drives stock prices higher. If the industry shows signs of sustained growth and aligns with a megatrend, this approach allows you to compound your investment over time.

By strategically *selling based on cost recovery, you mitigate the risk of a downturn while capitalizing on long-term growth opportunities.*

Remember, a megatrend could be a lifetime opportunity to multiply your investments.

Intentionally Left Blank

Rule No. 13:

Be Mindful of Frequent Trading.

An average trader often *develops habitual trading patterns* that are prone to mistakes, which can lead to capital risk. It also increases your trading costs.

Mindful trading is based on clear, factual data and tested strategies. It involves identifying large *price-value gaps* to protect your losses or allow you enough time to sell and correct mistakes.

You might have noticed that brokers often recommend buying stocks. This benefits brokers in two ways: a) they can earn large commissions from frequent trading, and b) since buyers will eventually need to sell, this assures second-leg of commissions to complete the trade.

Consequently, ***brokers tend to promote more buy recommendations than sell. So, be watchful about whom you are listening to and what could be their intention behind it!***

Excessive trading can dampen real returns, expose you to more mistakes, greater risks, and increase anxiety. Therefore, it is essential to manage your trading activity carefully <u>to stay in the game</u> for the long term.

Intentionally Left Blank

Rule No. 14:

Do Not Sell to Give Up Profits to Manage the Taxes.

In trading, it is essential to be mindful of capital gain taxes, as they are typically higher for short-term holdings than long-term ones. Short-term capital gains tax applies to stocks held under twelve months, while long-term gains benefit from lower tax rates.

When reviewing your trading report, you may identify low-probability trades or loss-making positions that could be adjusted for short-term gains. This adjustment can help reduce the overall tax burden for the financial year.

It is important to note that capital taxation rules vary by country.

In some jurisdictions, regulations allow you to carry forward losses from previous years to offset current gains. Understand these tax laws.

Therefore, strategizing your sales is crucial to managing taxes and timing effectively. This strategic approach makes you feel financially savvy and puts you in control of your tax liabilities, ensuring you do not pay more than necessary.

Generally, selling stocks solely to manage taxes is not advisable unless you are in a specific situation or have preplanned strategies to save a significant amount on tax costs.

*****

7 Conclusion

"What the wise do in the beginning, fools do in the end."

— Warren Buffett

An investor achieves success by selecting investments in strong businesses with capable management and knowing when it is most appropriate to buy or sell.

It is crucial to recognize the following facts about selling:

1. *Selling is riskier than buying*: Given the importance of capital compounding in wealth accumulation, selling poses greater risks.

2. *Selling is tactical.* A well-defined framework and strategy for selling can mitigate feelings of regret and enhance decision-making.

3. *Selling is tough.* No one knows what might emerge in the underlying business once you sell. A takeover or change in management has made many struggling companies bloom and created wealth for shareholders, such as Apple stock before Steve Jobs' return. Hence you need to have a critical view when selling.

4. Selling is art. Even though there are rules to follow, selling is more of an art form. Selling is the ultimate option. Use whatever is required with the right strokes. Play the game artfully.

5. *An investor* buys a piece of business to hold perpetually, with selling not in mind - unless there are two conditions: a) the breaking of the buy thesis (why it was bought) and/or b) an exceptionally better opportunity (high opportunity

cost). And many more rules as discussed earlier.

6. An investor is exposed to less risk because of: a) fewer transactions (no sell) or decisions to make, hence fewer mistakes; b) the strength of the underlying business gives comfort that stock price will follow value sooner or later; and c) optionally, a dividend is paid regularly to care for own cash flows.

7. *A trader* takes more risks by consistently hunting for bargains in the jungle (market). He must have a superior understanding of where to look for bargains and evaluate the price-value gap with margin-of-safety. They must make more buying, holding, and selling decisions, exposing themselves to more risk scenarios.

Finally, I strongly recommend having your sell framework and strategies in place. The world is full of opportunities, and the equity stock market is a wonderful platform to play the game.

Use ideas in this little book to prepare your own selling process and strengthen your investment and trading framework strategies.

Thank you for your attentive reading.

Best Wishes,

Balaji Kasal

info@balajikasal.com

*****

8 All Sell Rules in One Place

For your ease access and reference all the rules of investment and trading are listed below –

8.1 **Rules for Selling as an Investor**

1. Rule No. 1: Sell When You Discover the Buy Was a Mistake.

2. Rule No. 2: Sell Losers Sooner Rather Than Later.

3. Rule No. 3: Sell When There Is Permanent Deterioration in Business Economics.

4. Rule No. 4: Sell When There is Evidence or a Pattern of Suspicious Accounting or Fraudulent Activities.

5. Rule No. 5: Sell When Industry Disruption Occurs and the Company Fails to Adapt.

6. Rule No. 6: Sell When the Company Faces Frequent or Persistent Labor Issues.

7. Rule No. 7: Sell When Facing a Legal Tussle That Could Make the Business Unsustainable.

8. Rule No. 8: Sell When Management Exhibits Undesirable Behavior Toward the Business or Shareholders.

9. Rule No. 9: Sell When Management Starts Playing Adventurous Games That Harm Business Economics.

10. Rule No. 10: Sell When You Observe Suspicious or Unusual Insider Selling Activities.

11. Rule No. 11: Sell to Redeploy the Capital into an

Exceptionally Better Opportunity.

12. Rule No. 12: Sell to Rebalance the Business Portfolio... With Caution.

13. Rule No. 13: Sell a Growth Stock and Switch to a Dividend Stock.

14. Rule No. 14: Sell if Regular Dividends Are Eliminated or in a Reducing Trend.

15. Rule No. 15: Do Not Sell Based on Price Action or an Increase in the Stock Price.

16. Rule No. 16: Sell When You Need Money to Address Emergency Situation... as a Last Resort.

8.2 **Rules for Selling as a Trader**

1. Rule No. 1: Sell When the Stock Price Converges to the Intrinsic Value of the Business.

2. Rule No. 2: Sell When the Stock Prices Rise Too High in Comparison to Underlying Business Value. OR Sell When the Market is in a Bubble Phase.

3. Rule No. 3: Sell When an Anticipated Corporate Event Gets Materialized and the Stock Price Adjusted Accordingly.

4. Rule No. 4: Sell Based on Specific Corporate Actions.

5. Rule No. 5: Follow the Private Equity Formula to Sell.

6. Rule No. 6: Sell When Growth Stocks Stop Growing.

7. Rule No. 7: Sell Once the Stock Reaches Your Predefined Target Price.

8. Rule No. 8: Sell When the Stock Price is Clearly in a Downtrend.

9. Rule No. 9: Sell When the Stock Price Has Stagnated for a Long Time.

10. Rule No. 10: Sell When There is a Change in the Industry Economic Cycle in Which the Company Operates.

The following trading sell rules pertain to what you should avoid doing:

11. Rule No. 11: Do Not Sell in a Hurry.

12. Rule No. 12: Do Not Sell All of Your Holdings in a New Industry Opportunity – A Megatrend.

13. Rule No. 13: Be Mindful of Frequent Trading.

14. Rule No. 14: Do Not Sell to Give Up Profits to Manage the Taxes.

*****

9 Glossary of Specific Terms

- **Owner:** Who owns a piece of the business by holding the stocks.
- **Businessman:** A person who enjoys owning the business and doing all the activities to carry out affairs to get maximum economic and personal satisfaction (fulfillment).
- **Investor:** A person who intends to make rational decisions based on facts and the prospectuses of marketable securities by paying the price and, in return, expects to get value over a reasonable period.
- **Cigar-butt investor:** A trader trying to take advantage of the gap between market price and perceived value of the company (typically based on liquidating value).

- **Trader:** Follows the philosophy of buying low and selling high irrespective of underlying business/asset/securities irrespective of time of the day or week. For her or him, the price is everything.
- **Speculator:** A speculator operates as a trader with few conceived past beliefs and environment and hopes to always gain in any market.
- **Intrinsic Value:** The present value of the cash flows that a business is expected to generate during its remaining life, discounted at an appropriate rate.
- **Mark-to-Market MTM:** The accounting method measures the current value of a company's assets and liabilities.

*****

10 Bibliography

- Mr. Balaji Kasal, 'The Intelligent Investor's Approach to Risk Mastery' by Balaji Kasal, Published – September 2024.
- Prof. Benjamin Graham, The Intelligent Investor, 1949.
- Mr. Charlie Munger, Poor Charlie's Almanack: The Wit and Wisdom of Charles T. Munger 2005.
- Mr. Howard Marks, The Most Important Thing, 2018.
- Mr. Parag Parikh, Value Investing and Bchavioral Finance: Insights Into Indian Stock Market Realities, 2009.
- https://alpha-affairs.com/2022/02/28/reason-to-sell-find-aplenty/
- www.balajikasal.com
- https://www.concentus.com/great-investors-know-never-good-time-invest/

11 Book Series – "The Intelligent Investor's"

"Be a learning machine to evolve to achieve your maximum potential and dreams."

– *Balaji Kasal*

I am writing **"The Intelligent Investor's"** as a series of books to help you in your investment journey. These are niche topics and no-nonsense.

Book No. 1:

The Intelligent Investor's Mistakes: Warren Buffett

The book was **#1 New Release** on a leading USA platform in multiple categories: Investing Portfolio Management,

Private Equity, and Mutual Funds.

Synopsis:

The book is a collection of Buffett's 38 companies where he made mistakes of either commission or omission. Each chapter is a company or an industry written in a short story followed by Buffet's and Munger's quotes. The timeframe starts from 1965, when Buffett acquired Berkshire Hathaway Inc., till recently, in 2023. They are loaded with wisdom and fun to read.

The focus of the book is to help an investor to learn the following lessons –

1) **Investment Framework and Processes**
2) **Investment Strategies**
3) **Risk Management**
4) **Capital Allocation**
5) **Smart Diversification**
6) **Decision Making**

The whole book is written to help you become a better investor and guard against your own emotional biases. Learn to evaluate a company's economic outcome and competitive strength, how to think about the market price movement and much more. These valuable lessons unleash your potential to maximize profit and build wealth.

Get the Access Now:

1. Amazon Platform:
   https://relinks.me/B0CW1CKX8H
   QR-Scan:

2. Apple Books:
   https://relinks.me/6499439960

3. Other Platforms:
   https://books2read.com/u/b0MdJa

4. Audio Book @Kobo Walmart:
   https://shorturl.at/zSJiZ

Book No. 2:

The Intelligent Investor's Approach to Risk Mastery

The book is probably the first holistic risk mastery.

The book was the **#1 New Release** on a leading USA platform in the Risk Management and Mutual Funds categories.

In investment, the risk is inevitable, but its severity and

probability vary. The book empowers you to manage the risk to - ***1) minimize the losses and 2) weigh the opportunity cost to maximize Profits.*** Further, you can devise the framework and strategies to take on long-term investment success.

The book is divided into four parts –

1. **Transform your mindset** and emotional intelligence to master effective investment decisions.
2. **Dive deep into business and industry ecosystems** to determine long-term compounding cash flows.
3. **Empower you to choose the exceptional management** to care for your ownership interest.
4. **Recognize your edge to stand out from the crowd mentality** to spot profitable investments and trading opportunities.

Get the Access Now:

1. Amazon Platform: https://relinks.me/B0DF1M8V7L

    QR-Scan:

2. Apple Books:
   https://rxe.me/6689522091

3. Other Platforms:
   https://books2read.com/u/m2alod

4. Audio Book @Kobo Walmart:
   https://shorturl.at/P1O8Q

Book No. 3:

The Intelligent Investor's Art of Selling

The book you read.

The Intelligent Investors Hub

A community for you to learn investing to build enduring wealth.

Highlights:

1. **Learn:** Courses, live sessions and one-to-one coaching to mater the Stock market.
2. **Implement:** Own framework and strategies that suit you based on your own goals and risk appetites. In hackathon sessions you design own and get ideas on most important aspects of investments.
3. **Collaborate:** The community is a safe place to share and take a peaceful investment journey.

We understand the journey towards financial freedom is long. Hence, the membership is for a lifetime.

To explore The Intelligent Investors Hub Community visit us at:

www.intelligentinvestorshub.com

Scan QR Code:

******

www.ingramcontent.com/pod-product-compliance
Lightning Source LLC
Chambersburg PA
CBHW020654220526
45464CB00001B/425